Chicken Farmer
I Still Love You

Poems

Lana Hechtman Ayers

publishing

Copyright © 2007 by Lana Hechtman Ayers

All rights reserved. No part of this work may be used or reproduced in any manner whatsoever without written permission from the publisher, except in the case of brief quotations embodied in critical articles and reviews.

ISBN 978-1-890424-49-7

Composed in Adobe Minion Pro with Scala Sans display at Hobblebush Books, Brookline, New Hampshire (www.hobblebush.com)

Cover photograph by Sidney Hall Jr.

Printed in the United States of America

Robert Hinson, *Publisher*
Witt Wittmann, *Editor*

D-N Publishing
598 INDIAN TRAIL ROAD S. #111
INDIAN TRAIL, NC 28079

*Copies of this book may be obtained
from D-N Publishing:* dnpemail@aol.com

in loving memory of my father,
Max Hechtman,
who believed in me
no matter what I did or didn't

I have found the paradox, that if you love until it hurts, there can be no more hurt, only more love.

— MOTHER TERESA

Contents

How to Fix a Flat

Acknowledgments

The author thanks the following presses for honoring her poems (sometimes in earlier versions) with publication: *Bellowing Ark* for "Honeysuckle" and "Maybe Love is More Like an Onion." *Bent Pin* for "Paris 1932." *Cadillac Cicatrix* for "Donald Couldn't Stop Thinking About Those Darn Pumpkins," "Easy As Pie" and "Love Is a Weed." *Color Wheel* for "Coltrane's 'Soul Eyes'." *Court Green* for "Clip Coupons and Save." *Dos Passos Review* for "Birthday." *Eating Pure Light: An Homage to Thomas McGrath* and *The Making of Peace Broadside Series* for "The Night Our Troops Invade." *The Henniker Review* for "The Dead Man and Haystacks." *Illya's Honey* for "After 'Finding a Long Gray Hair'." *Kean Review* for "Triptych of Heaven." *Lake Effect* for "Dorothy Does Italy" and "In the Move, George Bailey Jumped." *Manorborn* for "Snow." *The Mochila Review* for "On Cue." *Natural Bridge* for "Sweet Stalk, an Elegy for Gwendolyn Brooks." "Poetry Jumps Off the Shelf" for "Nonfat Decaf Love" under the title "Blind Love" as a java jacket. Poery365.com for "Easy As Pie." *Poetry Super Highway* for "Do Not Mistake Heaven for What Descends." *Rhino* for "The Paradox of Life and Religion." *Silk Road* for "How to Fix a Flat." *Snap* for "Diner Waitress," "What the Roof Hears at Night" and "'Chicken Farmer I Still Love You'." *Stimulus Respond* for "Adaptation in the Motor City," "How Red Light Swings," "Lipstick" and "Trapped." *StringTown* for "Algebra," "Pass Work" and "Waiting." *Town Creek Poetry* for "Whisper, He's Driving." *Umbrella* for "After Sex." *West Wind Review* for "Screen Door To the Sea." *White Pelican Review* and *Letters To the World Anthology* for "Near Winter Solstice." The Woman Made Gallery *2008 Her Mark Calendar* for "Because God Doesn't Have Wings." Additionally, "Fairy Tale Affair," "Love at the El Al Check-In Counter," "Love Is a Weed," "Love Trips," "Midday Tuesday," "Shut Up and Drive" and "Whisper, He's Driving" appeared in the chapbook *Love Is a Weed*, published in 2006 by Finishing Line Press.

Sincere thanks to D-N Publishing, Robert Hinson, Ph.D. and Sharyn Witt Wittmann for selecting my manuscript as winner of their National Full-Length Poetry Book Competition. And heartfelt thanks to Sidney Hall Jr. for another wonderful book design, and to Kayt Hoch for her cover ideas and restoration of the photo on the back cover. Warm thanks to all my colleagues and mentors who supported and encouraged this collection of poems, especially the members of Poets Unbound, the Striped Water Poets, the woman of V-6, Rane Arroyo, Marvin Bell, Joan Larkin, Anne Marie Macari, Paulann Peterson, Cecilia Woloch and Carolyne Wright. Special thanks to the Hedgebrook Foundation for a generous residency during which I put the finishing touches on this manuscript. Convivial thanks to Rosina Johnson, Newbury, NH town librarian and Maureen Rosen for help with my research. Deep gratitude to my loved ones, too numerous to mention here (you know who you are!), whose affectionate support sustains me on a daily basis. Last, but never least, loving thanks to my third grade teacher Mrs. Sarfaty for kissing fuchsia lipstick wings on my cheek and dubbing me a poet.

CHICKEN FARMER I STILL LOVE YOU

Easy As Pie

To live in this world you must be able to do three things:
to love what is mortal;
to hold it against your bones knowing your own life depends on it,
and, when the time comes to let it go, to let it go.

— MARY OLIVER

"Chicken Farmer I Still Love You"

Graffiti on a granite boulder along SR 103 in Newbury, NH

This life that evaporates like rain
asks only that you bend
to kiss the dirt once in a while.

Give thanks for the holiness of gravity's hold,
the plain-elegant truth of standing,
feeling the pull from your soles of your feet
up through your marrowbones
to the narrow isle of corpus callosum
in your brain.

Each diminutive cell of your body
is its own hive,
a place of jasmine and moonlight,
a place of sun and postcards.

Every day, breathe in deeply,
breathe all the way to your toes,
the pregnant sky.

Let not a week pass without
sucking your fingers clean
for sweetness.

Amid feed corn and feathers,
amid confusion and doubt,
dare your heart into words—
Chicken farmer I still love you!

Remember that love
is as unstoppable as granite,
even if it was never
meant to be.

Nonfat Decaf Love

In the café, awaiting your venti latte,
why not take a moment to admire someone
whose identity will remain a secret even to you?

Go ahead, scribble a love note (or make it two)
and bury it in the stack of counter napkins—
Baby, you jump-start my heart like double espresso!

This world doesn't care a hill of decaffeinated beans
for the troubles of any two coffee lovers.
Your billet-doux will deftly sweeten the brew.

Easy As Pie

I don't know how many hungers there are . . .
— Kim Addonizio

All day I've been reading poems about
unfinished conversations,
unanswered prayers,
a woman fed up with how
people die so horribly and live
without ever finding lasting love,

and in the middle, there's this amazing image—
pies spinning in the glass refrigerator case
of a restaurant,
long after it's closed.

The diner heaven of Astoria, Queens
where I was raised,
was a haven for those brightly-lit,
spinning showrooms—
blueberry, rhubarb and apple pies,
foot-high strawberry shortcake,

Devil's Tower chocolate,
cheesecakes topped with cherry glaze,
éclairs chubby as newborns,
ruby and emerald cubed Jell-O's.

So many magnificent choices—
a jewel case for desire.
Wouldn't it be grand
if love could be like that,
where the only trouble—the only one—
is which sweet thing to pick?

And yet,
whether you're the type
who savors or the type who gobbles,
it all ends up devoured, disappeared, gone.

What you're left with is
"can't-believe-I-ate-the-whole-thing" guilt
and heartburn,
which pass,
but those love handles,
those extra dollops

of cream on your hips,
baby, let me tell you,
easy as pie,
those will last you your whole life.

Donald Couldn't Stop Thinking About Those Darn Pumpkins

Rolling New England hills,
house on five wooded acres,
enclosed swimming pool, the dream
Donald's best friend was selling,
of perfect union,
a boy, a girl, a Golden Retriever.

The blind date his best friend
had set him up with
was already half an hour late,
and the dream was getting
harried, more like late-night
infomercial by the second.

All Donald could think about was,
not whether his date would be pretty,
not even if she would like him,
not if she would put out,
but what if those rolling New England hills
were all covered with pumpkins,

and what if great winds came along,
and the pumpkins begin to roll,
and the rolling gathered such momentum,
those pumpkins became orange tanks,
and what if at the bottom of one of those hills
sat a lone tomcat, happily licking its paw?

Honeysuckle

After William Stafford

After you look into his two brown eyes,
the moon will lose its appeal,
less mysterious for being a single glow.

After you look and his two brown eyes
look back into yours,
your heart's drumming will set the sky to music.

One of you will mention weather,
clouds shaped like teapots.

One of you will whistle,
warm sting of blood flowing into your cheeks,
sunrise from inside the body.

You will point to a flower,
call it, wrongly, honeysuckle.

Both of you will laugh and chatter until
one of you hears a voice calling like arctic winds
from across continents, across oceans.

Then you will part forever.
Years later,

you will dream the earth has two moons
and you will rise from your bed in the night,
go outside to see if it isn't so.

Love Is a Weed

Wish still on the stem,
I'm driving away from you,
crossing myself
that disaster isn't around the next curve.

My foot is atomic
on the gas pedal,
car guzzling its beer-gold ambrosia.
Scenery passes, night hawks take wing.

Deer caught in the headlight stare
is only me,
checking myself in the rearview.
Will you ever commit?

I'm cruising the brain's map of paradise,
close to empty.
I'm searching for Daddy
in the dusty stars of heaven, just rising.

The moon's wearing her
"Do Not Disturb" albatross,
so who can I ask
why *uno* is not many?

There's nothing I can do about
the time-lock on your heart.
Or about Atlas, hurling away the world.
Like you my love, he's all man.

Oh, if only I could blow dandelion smoke
into your eyes, crack the safe.
I'd turn cartwheels inside your skin
and throw away the key.

Midday Tuesday

Like a trapped sparrow,
light flutters around
inside the tunnel-toddling
subway car.

We've all entered willingly.
Two men in suits point
to an article in the *Wall Street Journal.*
One laughs.

I am feeling the emptiness
of the seat next to me.
This absence has a name,
I just don't know it yet.

Directly across,
a woman with deep-furrowed skin
knits her pale hands.
The seat next to her is empty too.

Soon I will arrive at a station where
red can be exchanged for green.
The inner life is not like this.
One voice can flip

the walls of your heart into doors.
Yesterday I asked
the Magic Eight Ball
if my man will always love me.

Without a doubt.
That's as good a test of faith as I know.
Maybe before I get home,
I'll buy a lottery ticket.

The subway screeches,
sidles into a shock of fluorescence.
One laughs.
So do I.

Birthday

After the painting by Marc Chagall

Lover, so flexible,
he's levitating above your lips,
head literally bent over backwards
to surprise your mouth with his.

He is like a swimming dolphin,
hovering above you in the yellow
underwater glow of the room.
You too begin to pitch forward,

your whole body willing
to fall into the seduction
of floating on air;
willing to leave gravity behind

for the two fish of your mouths,
the wet press of warm gills,
breathing air like water.
There is no contortion more natural

than the buoyancy of desire.
In this red-carpeted room
the air is parting,
like the sea of Moses,

holding aloft special passage
for two bodies
to give birth
to salt.

After Sex

It's 3AM,
you outside for the last
cigarette before bed,

me along for company,
making breath angels.
You making angels

of smoke and breath both,
yours more
ethereal.

In porchlight
your face is luminous
as if wet.

The sky too cloudy
for stars, I look
up into your eyes,

see a country there
you visit
without me,

one that borders
the coal-eyed moon,
requires

a passport
of silence.
I don't ask

if it's warmer there.
I know not to expect
a postcard.

Lipstick

The magician's assistant is psychic and wears blue,
the color of pure thought.

She lusts after my man, and
intuits a golden key to his apartment door.

While he's sleeping, she lets herself in,
curls up in his brown corduroy slippers.

She never stops brushing her fingers
through his thick black hair,

even while we're crossing a crowded intersection
and the light turns red.

My man smokes his Camels.
He's close-lipped.

I fear he's already making it with her
in the black top hat of his mind—

the one place I can't ransack,
expose her paranormal *Lava Dew* lipstick smears.

Victim

I love you, she says.
"So," he says.

Mean, she says.
He laughs.

She leaves the room and comes back.

"Where'd you get that axe?" he asks.
I love you, she says.

"I love you," he says.
So, she says.

"So keep away with that axe," he says.
She laughs.

Fairy Tale Affair

How does it go?
Thick black hair on his chest, tight buttocks,
eyes bluer than wedlock.

I'd like to tell you conversation sparked it all—
his deep listening, my wit.
Really, just a wand in the right place.

His body, glass-sleek, perfect fit
for my Cinderella midlife crisis.
We rode that carriage around and around the block.

At home, I turned back into pumpkin piety
Then evil sister-in-law rats me out to hubby.
How does it end?

Palace of divorce court, half of nothing,
and my prince takes off
with some sugar god-momma.

Sisters all, the moral: beware those glitzy glass slippers.
They hobble ever after
the heart of the wearer.

On Cue

This story's clean as
the zygote gleam

in your mother's eye
when she lay with your father

on the pool table
in the after-hours bar,

lifted her flouncy skirt,
lowered her cotton bloomers

to offer him something more fragrant
than a ninety-nine cent beer.

Oh, oh, oh! she exclaimed,
the green felt burning her bottom raw.

Behind more than the eight-ball
when the rabbit croaked,

your daddy passed his honeymoon night
passed-out under a barstool,

and your mommy, clutching her abdomen,
in the ladies room throwing up.

Some say it was the cheap draft.
Others, the pied eyes of fate.

But any priest will sanctify it
a blessing with two gold rings,

belly-full for Jesus,
the bride all dressed in white,

pure as soap
stirred in the ash-pot.

Maybe Love Is More Like an Onion

He says he loves me and keeps reading the sports section.
I say to him, *Passion is a budding rose.*
"Spring training is almost over," he says.
Green, guarded at first,
then explosive—bursting, brilliant, sensual, perfumed.
He turns a page. "Bruins are down to fifth in the division," he says.
Petals so soft, they make you cry, I say. *Opening further, further.*
"That reminds me," he says, "we need toilet paper."
The color fades, I say.
"Then buy the white," he says.
The petals wrinkle, drop, leave just a shaft of thorns.
He says, "Got to call my mother today."
I say, *Compost.*

Token

Like strangers on a subway
the husband and wife sit on the sofa,
facing the window of the television,
its screenlight flickering,
volume turned down so low
speech is insensible,
stations sliding by while they
wait to see which of them will get off first.

Pass Work

Like the rest of us, I rent time;
take up my spot in the designated bed
on the designated street
in the dwelling numbered 4-1-1
but no one's giving out any good information here;
the usual TV rackets with blue glare,
the dishwasher gargles
glasses past midnight.

        I wasn't born into this life
        or was I,
        all pink-faced
        with a mouth ready to suck
        on rubber tips
        since a mother who was breast dry.

& I've always wondered if it's true an angel
kisses the knowledge out of babies
putting a light-rayed fingertip to the top lip
and whispering it into the bow-curved shape
of heart with the command "forget."

If so, I forgot it all
and never will remember
no matter how many apples I bite down.

        Truth's a joker
        that could stand in for any suit.
        Like any suit & tie John
        that walks in the double-barreled
        door at ten past,
        swinging technology onto the table
        with a what's-for-dinner-smile.

& would I even want more than this?
I'm anybody's Eve or
everybody's,
though sometimes my name is
merely Ma'am.

I miss "Miss,"
shed a droopy-eyed tear for it.
Sleep catches all my sins
and spins them into riddles,
what if's.

Mornings, the sun measures
my determination, and falling shy,
I dab an extra dab of artful
rouge to the cheeks.

Neighbors' dogs keep on barking
at imagined trespass
and I zip myself closed, as required,
quiet for the ride.
You can't sell what was never
yours but somehow,
we all do.

Shut Up and Drive

The moon's a stubbed big toe
in twilight's bruised sky.

I'm glaring at you with my tequila eye,
the other's making sure we don't miss our exit.

A few more miles till sun-up. We've but this one
car and behind us, exhaust.

Love Trips

Every time I'm rushing to unfold a map
it seems some man's
the reason I'm lost—
a typical man who won't ask directions
or is so attracted by billboard signs,
he falls for all their false turns.

So we end up taking turns
studying the mangled map,
turning it around, looking desperately for a sign
to direct us back from the no-man's
land of changed direction,
the unmarked road where we strayed to end up lost,

though he won't admit to being lost.
We take one hundred eighty degree turns
blaming each other in directionless
arguing and of course the map's
no use to "I've got a natural sense of direction"-man
who says it's my fault anyway for making him miss the sign.

Was there even a sign
to miss? How do we lose
that initial spark so easily, the flawless man
I thought he was at first just turns
into another version of Daddy and I'm the perfect map
of my mother, buttoning my lip by direction

of the man at the helm, following the direction
of his life, an "I'm only the passenger sign"
practically tattooed to my forehead, with map-
like furrows highlighting my lost
enthusiasm for this latest one-eighty turn
of events and I know I should know by now that no man

can bring the happiness I always look for in a man.
Inevitably in relationships, all roads go only one direction:
south. Some take the scenic route, but finally there's the turn-
off that veers from pavement to muddy potholes. One-way signs
appear: late nights at the office, turning away in bed, lost
interest in sex, conversation skills of a turtle. There is no map

that can route me back to my ideal man, just a dead-end sign.
Time for a new direction. In love and travel, once again, I've lost.
Instead of another wrong turn, I'll get a *GPS*, swear off driving with men.

Traveler's Tautology

If you can't live in the moment,
you will never arrive
where you are.

Love at the El-Al Check-In Counter

After Maria Negroni's "Infinite Dictionary"

Airline employee what it means to rent creativity His olive face dark eyes black hairs on his arms not tenderness but something more insidious His words entrance visa You're used to flying American no fear of water landing but crave turbulence accustomed to bumps Did he say no seatbelt You say boarding pass Hesitation This isn't a marriage His gaze Mediterranean his lips the lullaby you awoke from Hard to grasp hoist your broken handled baggage inside computer documents you saved He backspaces deletes You love him like omission Pompeii blind rage Speak friction to him How you hardly breathe under his weight scream then turn away He hasn't been listening You the fool who makes up for customs Employees resign are fired He's amused When you left Egypt he's saying to the new blonde obviously lost His smile the gate number you need to get off Did you forget how wind hides in a painted canvas recall ravens lifting from your eyes realize the sanguine night manager asleep in your hands His good-humored glance sends flame Salamanders dancing on the moon Love is the infinite dictionary but in all translations is synonymous with end

In the Movie, George Bailey Jumped

I.

For you, my real-life George, I hog-tied the moon
to the old silver maple out back.
Of course, the moon broke the rope,
kept on rising anyway.
I should've known better—
the moon's such a guileful gal,
going up to flash her powder-keg eyes
at all the other guys in the world.

You settled for my buffalo smile.

II.

There isn't any stork who brings babies,
though we've tried to lasso it.

Your elevator may go all the way up
to the top of my building and loan,

but your sperm
no longer drop the shaft.

You say the whole in-vitro thing
is for the birds.

Only an angel can help us now.

III.

In my dreams the world is
a post-apocalyptic Pottersville,
all seedy bars and live nudie shows.

Instead of your ex-wife, I'm Violet,
pushing fifty, lipstick bleeding the cracked corners
of my deflated pout.

I'm still looking for a good time
but not even the sailors on leave are buyin'.
Sometimes I'll get a pity-dime;

mostly I don't even get a match for my cigarette.
When I wake up,
not much is different except

I've got my own lighter.

Clip Coupons and Save

It's already June
and all those fences remain unmended. Stress
is a cycle as contiguous as the tide-pull of moon.
How not to obsess

over time's snake-
like slithering ways, making intention moot
until there's nothing to eat but ache? Cake
was Antoinette's beaut

of an answer. Garbo
was better off mute, her eyes an enigmatic play
of shadow and seduction. Ask any shopping cart hobo
what makes his day:

a doorway to stay dry, a bottle to stay wet. Rings of rhinestone
sun-blind any fool's eyes. Rain is awfully economical cologne.

Paradise Is Always Greener

God says to Eve, "That snake that lies
in the grass is harmless.

It is good, green and wholesome
and will mind its own business

if you keep to your own affairs."
And Eve, being Eve, and knowing

it's best to appease the male egos
around her, says, "Sure thing, God.

By the way, Adam's looking for you.
Apparently he's tangled up his tinkler

in some vines and can't seem to
figure out how to free himself."

"That's my boy," God says,
disappearing, his beard becoming

just another fluffy cumulus.
As soon as Eve is certain God's

good and gone, she goes off
looking for some slippery snake

action in the green grass.
She's in the mood to harass.

Why Things Don't Fall Apart

There are three wise men in my kitchen.
All day they eat oranges, spit the seeds,
throw peels on the floor.

They drink.
They smoke.
They swear.

But I don't toss them out the door.
That would leave me only
the moon to argue with.

Did It Come True?

The heart is the only broken instrument that works.

— T. E. KALEM

What Bugs Me

For Tim Seibles

For Bugs Bunny, I sat so close, my nose
practically pressed into the screen.
It was a thrill to be the first one awake,
to race to the TV and click it on to see his face.
He was my prince, my knight, my dreamboat.

I copied him, ate carrots by the bunch,
his favorite food, and for years,
he duped me into rooting for the winner
because he won, because he was fleeter,
quicker to the punch,

because he could pull anything out of a hat—
the kitchen sink, a rifle, a five-course
meal complete with table and chair,
a candelabra and violinist, even himself.
Trouble didn't happen to him—

he invented it, sought it out, thrived on it.
Did anyone for a moment think of the poor, dull
woodsman, likely with a wife and starving children,
just trying to bag one meager meal?
And what about the black mallard

who could never measure up
and finally turned to greed, craved
material possessions to try to fill
the impossible (nonexistent) shoes
of the big-eared, lucky-footed hero?

How could I have been so naïve to root
for the one left standing, the one
kicking the loser when he was down?
Just because he was clever and cute,
because he looked equally comely in

a pair of heels and a dress
as in a top-hat and tux,
because he could dance better than
Fred Astaire or Ginger while filing his nails.
Maybe he was supposed to be

innovative, represent tenacious spirit,
indomitable will. Over the years
I found out how many true-to-character
Bugses there are in the world outside the TV—
clean-looking, fast-talking, sure-footed.

They'll kick your teeth down your throat
while wearing a *What's Up, Doc?* smile
and you won't ever see it coming.
Even now, audiences are laughing.
Those Bugses send us Elmer Fudds of the world

home to lick our wounds, egg on our faces.
Cartoons *are* exactly like real life—the winner isn't
always the good guy but pretends he is just the same.
Thanks, charming Bugs, for a lesson learned late.
At least all those carrots didn't do me any harm.

Ode To Bogart

Diminutive Humphrey had me spellbound.
Scowling and wise-cracking his way around
the ladies, leaving them utterly disarmed,
charmed, adoring, defenseless,
while he fist-fought his way through the goons,
favoring the sound of a good skin-on-skin crack
to the loud racket of a gun.

He cracked the whip of his wit and mind, as well,
skirting blind-alleys, unwinding minotaur maze-like plots,
and unpuzzling every mystery by the end.
Though sometimes, he was the gangster goon himself,
heartless and harrowing, but slick as spit,
and twice as smooth, sucking in butts
and blowing his own smoky aura.

Even when he was bad, the broads wanted him bad,
went for him, though they never would swear to it in court,
not the sort to cavort and tell.
And Humphrey's guise was never the kind of guy
who was shy about smacking a dame who gave him lip,
she had it coming, same as the rest.
Knock 'em to the floor and they'd be back for more.

He was the hero that proved the little guy's no ant,
and you can't stop freedom, especially if it's for France.
Even with the heat of the cops breathing down his neck
or a heater pointed right on him, he belted attitude,
Come and get me copper, What's a matter, ya yellow?
Is it any wonder I wanted a fellow like Humphrey?
The stuff that dreams are made of.

Now, my wisecracking man gives me a whack to the jaw
and I'm a regular Mary Astor. So what if there's more
violence than romance, the falcon's made of lead,
and he double-crosses me in another woman's bed?
In life's movie, pain's the plot thickener, sweetheart,
and you'll always have Paris and one great theme song.
You know how to whistle it, don't you?

Dorothy Does Italy

Once bitten, the travel bug stayed with her,
and she traded gusting dust storms
for jet streams and skipped the stratosphere
to emeraldine cities across the globe.
Right now she's in Venice (not the one in Nebraska)
discovering the putrid pungency of canals omitted by
those travel brochures' four-color pitch for romance.
Always there's a catch, she thinks, *the stinker behind the curtain.*

Even so she considers the Gondolas graceful and imagines
a postcard of courageous Toto (long dead, buried) riding head high
at the heel of a boat, barking for joy into the witchy fog.
Jolted from her reverie by a timid waiter with tin-blue eyes,
she nods *yes* for another espresso and wonders if tonight's the night
her ruby dancing shoes will raise one hell of a memorable gale.

Alice's Blind Date with Frankenstein's Monster

Where the personal ad read, *tall,*
Alice assumed *dark and handsome.*
Where it read, *Loves moonlit walks through the cemetery,*
Alice surmised, *romantic.*
And the bit, *Firebugs need not apply,*
she thought quirky charm.

So what harm could come by answering?
Only that learning reality is a bitter cake
that sometimes shrinks one's hopes.
That he wasn't handsome,
was an understatement.
But in his favor, he had a friendly laugh

and looked deeply into Alice's eyes.
He didn't bat an eyelash (in fact he had none to bat)
at her whole *Looking Glass* story
the way her parents had upon her return,
then sent her to bed without supper yet again.
The cemetery her blind date picked for their picnic

was wide and well-lit under the full moon
and though he was creepily patched
from mismatched skins of the dead,
his green pallor glowed a warmer hue.
He wore his fears on his ragged sleeve:
fire, villagers, dogs, and shed a few tears

telling her of his longing for a true companion.
He wasn't the worst date she'd ever had.
Also, he seemed to completely grasp
yearning for wholeness, the very thing
Alice herself wanted but had not the words to express
since the incidents with the older gentleman

that began when she was only six.
Her truth was that monsters
don't always look the part.

Those that do can turn out not frightening at all
and can have quite a good heart
(even if electric shock is necessary to get it started).

Frank, he'd asked her to call him,
just *Frank*, and not wanting to wait
for things between them to cool too much
she did when she rang
him up the very next day
to ask him out on a second date.

Vigil

After Stuart Dybek

On a cobbled lane stained
by the flashbulb blood of angels,
I thought I saw your body floating,
stripped to the waist in the moist air.
I cataloged the architecture
of your laugh on the downdraft.
Who else could that silhouette
mimic when, by the licking tongues
of ashcan vigil flames kissing the cold
hands of homeless men, you drifted?
From the after-hours nightclub
the racked myopic eyes
of shotglasses squinted
through tinted barroom glass.
With each sweep of your arms
your carriage, blurred but ever
beguiling, evanesced
up the sainted alley of cathedrals,
and raising my beer, I recalled
the scent of your flesh
doppelgangered by the incense
of a musky Catholic confessional
dewy with sweat.

Paris 1932

After a photograph by Gilberte Brassai

Flannel mist enwraps *Avenue de L'Observatoire.*
Bare oaks marble the sky,
streetlamps like lowered moons, patient the distance.

It's late, the newsstand is closed,
and the lone man sitting across from it
tries to light a damp cigarette.

Sporting a gray raincoat and black fedora, the man, murky
in the legerdemain of shadow and lens, will remain
on this city bench eternally parted from the woman he desires

who's rising from her make-up table in an elegant boudoir
on the *Rue Magnifique* in Paris, 1932,
slipping his gift of a dragon-embroidered, red Chinese silk robe

off her shoulders, letting it puddle to the glossy wooden floor.
Candle glow brocades her skin as she glissades bright lemon
slices across her throat and bosom in anticipation of his arrival.

The lone man's cigarette finally catches.
He drops the match to the wet ground, smoke from his mouth
mingling undetectably with foggy night air, and he whistles lightly.

Guernica, April 27, 1937

*On April 27, 1937, Adolf Hilter's air force bombed the Basque
village of Guernica for target practice. It was a market day.
Approximately 1,654 people were murdered and 889 injured.*
— *Guernica, A Magazine of Art & Politics*

By the gate, Enrique,
still in his good market clothes,
waits for an answer.
Not used to waiting
he bounces on the balls
of his feet.
Carmen has turned
her face toward the road
to watch shoppers
heading home with
brimming baskets of produce.
A sudden wind brings
the scent of *Narcissus Triandrus,*
Angel's tears,
and lifts Carmen's hair,
dark as crow wings.
In the distance an odd
brassy sound, someone
playing a horn, badly?
Carmen laughs, modestly
covering her mouth.
Enrique, not laughing,
impatient, slaps his thigh,
seizes Carmen by the shoulders,
turning her towards him.
Her laughter disappears
into his moustache
as he kisses her.
Carmen's eyes wide open,
her neck tilts back
swooning into her first kiss
and she sees
the sky breaking into dark shapes,
immense *cigarras*
floating down to earth.

The Night Our Troops Invade

Believing myself a citizen of peace,
I go outside to commune with the stars.
A handful, squeezed between tall dwellings,
blink, inscrutable as the Great Sphinx,
older than any human nation.

I wonder about all those dark years,
the millions of years light traveled
to reach my eyes at this very moment,
all the lives that rose and fell therein,
undocumented, ungrieved.

My reverie is broken by the eerie calls
of Cuckoos, nocturnal invaders,
parasitic birds who abandon their young
to the nests of other species,
devoid of basic maternal instinct.

The blinking stars, those blind historians,
beg this riddle: how we finite creatures,
lucky to have been given life in a universe
of infinite void, can fail to love every
being whose eyes reflect back into our own?

Do Not Mistake Heaven for What Descends

In a small village outside Baghdad,
a house with an earthen floor
is filled with the morning music
of children's chatter

and the chiming of hand forged spoons
against handmade clay bowls.
A little girl in a yellow dress
burns her tongue on a bit of hot grains.

Her adolescent brother with a cricket voice
sings about the size of his sister's nose,
teasing her that it is so large it can be seen
from heaven itself.

He pulls her long dark hair until
a few strands let go and the girl cries out.
The mother scolds that brother
in a language that sounds like

the chopping of almonds.
Meanwhile, the younger brother,
whose eyes are the sweet brown of dates,
sits in a corner silent, watching a spider

weave a glistening bridge from wall to wall.
Just then, a stray missile fired by our side
descends near the two-room house.
In the flash of moment before the family

is overcome by heat and by smoke,
they witness the intense burning of the roof,
and the youngest brother wonders if
the sun felt so tired that it fell from the sky.

To W.

I've read the last page of the bible. It's all
going to turn out all right.
—Billy Graham

If my heart were more than flesh,
if flesh were more than time,
if time were more than imaginary,
if the imaginary was God
and God was flesh,
then he could walk with you
in this ruined countryside,
this country ruined
by the handiwork
of your words,
and if words were more than faith,
if faith was more than fear,
(and fear less than failure),
then God could grant you forgiveness
for what you've done,
but I would rather my flesh,
my heart still beating in my chest,
be consumed by maggots,
than grant you mine.

How Red Light Swings

Red light swings into afternoon in the yard
that is unwalked by anyone but the neighbor's
one-eyed alley cat and a few brown squirrels.
Leaves blow around, catch in chain-link.

I am standing by the draft over my kitchen sink
looking at what the wind translates
into movement of gray branches,
a sign language the robins know.

Sound bleeds my ears from the bedroom TV—
gunshots, sirens,
bad drama imitating a life
no one of us would choose if given choice.

This waiting is dust—precursor to dehydrated cells.
If the water in every human body
were suddenly to disperse
the oceans would double in size.

I heard that on NPR maybe, maybe made it up.
Later, I will check the front door I already know
is locked, and after,
when red light swings to the blackest dream

of black outside these walls, I'll lie awake
holding the ghost of love in my arms,
staring at a ceiling where, if I could, I'd imagine stars.
I'd god-up a whole sky,

a sky without planets,
a sky with nothing but suns
scorching themselves out of existence,
all blue flame and gardenia-white fury.

But for now, I watch how red light swings
into the unwalked yard, and beyond,
across timeless distance,
like the singing crown of desire, made visible.

Near Winter Solstice

A man stands in his yard facing
the gradient of pine
that eventuates to deep woods.

A quiet night as always
in this far from city-lights hamlet.
Cold, but not unpleasant.

The ice in the glass he's holding
rasps, sighs.
He tilts back a long swallow.

The sky has the deep sheen
of crafted mahogany, the stars
are a multitude of fine crystal bells

he can almost hear
summoning him.
Inside the house

there will be cake,
trick candles, singing.
There will be flowing wine,

companionable words.
Soon he will join his party,
but for now he's thinking

about the wind,
how its voice
through the tall dry grass

on this clearest of eves,
sounds so much like rain, so much
like want.

Diner Waitress

Air conditioning on the fritz
that the boss won't fix,
Summer exhausts her,
sweat swaddling her middle-aged body.

Once voluptuous so many springs ago,
desire was the flavor of the moment,
and desperate hands on moonlit nights
grabbed for hidden sources of heat.

Head cheerleader, her pompommed embraces
reached out to the lucky few:
the pipe-necked track star
she watched from the back of a motorcycle

wrap a tree around his skull;
the blue-eyed football captain
who called the plays
and left her pregnant under the stands.

Now there are frying pans under her eyes,
shoulder blades jut out of her back
like bony handles to the double doors of her spine.
Open her up, and you'd find nothing but grizzle.

She wipes a stain on the Formica lunch counter
that's been there for years,
her veiny hand making geometric swipes
as if she's spelling out a cheer.

At night, waiting up for
her own teenaged daughter
she soaks her blistered feet in Epsom,
lets a cigarette dangle from her mouth.

In the diary she keeps in her head
she writes this:
> Spring withers from these bones
> like the orange weeping of tulips.

Whisper, He's Driving

A gray chamois shawl enwraps the morning sky.
She's thinking of what her grandma used to say
whenever it rained like this,
"It's a good day to be a fish," and she smiles.
For a moment, she studies him, his hands knuckled

to the steering wheel, then closes her eyes. The downpour
against the windshield sounds something like November
leaves crushed underfoot, like oil spattering from a pan,
but reminds her most of the clatter
of her string of cobalt glass beads,

broken, scattering across the oaken floor,
last night, when he hit her but didn't mean to,
his hand a blunt board,
his ring snaring the clasp, tearing
the whole thing from her throat.

This weather shushes her heart, that she imagines
glows with smudgy incandescence inside her chest,
much like the blurred necklace of halted taillights ahead.
"Could a person drown in all this rain?"
she wonders aloud, but softly,

whisper, he's driving.
Around the shoulders of the highway,
she sees that all the maple trees are bare but one,
one still clutching clusters of leaves, yellow bouquets
like roses one offers in sympathy.

Commandment VII

Little things did not add up—
travel times, crumbs, receipts.
Callers not leaving messages.
A bra in the dryer, not hers.
She understood this

to be her own paranoia.
It was a laundromat after all.
How could he love her
and not be faithful?
It wasn't in him,

he told her.
Better to understand
little things did not add up
because they never did.
Once, with a friend,
she saw from a distance

a man in a trench coat
light a cigarette
then place it in a woman's mouth.
The gesture made her cold all over
because it was his gesture.

So she came to understand
all men in trench coats,
lighting cigarettes,
were him.
This eased her mind.

Only finding the wet jacket
continued to disturb her—
soaking wet—
on the back seat of his car.
It hadn't rained in days.

A quick wash to remove
the scent of perfume, of sex?
Eventually she came to understand
it must have rained,
he caught

in a downpour or the jacket left
by an open window in his car.
It was not lent to another woman,
though all women
shivering in the rain, were her.

Which Mistake?

A man turns a corner and does not look back.

Spode wedding china slowly returns to clay on a back porch he walked out of.

Rusty the Irish Setter's ears prick up when cars with the same tread of tires as the man's sough up the street.

A nameless pink teddy bear's face is wet with the man's daughter's tears.

There are names for what the man has done to his family, most of them ugly.

The man is in love again, or maybe for the first time, he thinks.

This is only good and right. Everyone goes on with their lives.

The man tries to say something pretty as moonlight to the new pretty girl he's with.

He tickles her foot. He kisses a toe.

Alice, he begins to say, which is of course, not her name.

The man laments out loud, Sorry, I've made a mistake.

Questions, extra credit:

What is the pretty girl's name? What is the daughter's name?
Why? Defend your answers.

What is the wife's name?
Did the pink teddy bear really have no name?

True or False: The moral is look both ways before crossing.

Tie-breaker: What is the ugliest name in the English language?

Tabloid

After "Poem" by Frank O'Hara

Frank O'Hara has climbed to the top
of the Empire State Building.
I was shopping at Macy's
and suddenly heard shouting
and panic from the streets
and you said it must be terrorists again.
Even half a dozen years after, I can taste
some bitter ash in the city air
and I try to tell myself it is a magician's illusion.
The flowers aren't there, the towers are.
Or else, I imagine you and I have been transported
back to the attic days of 1933
and we look up to see FRANK O'HARA HAS CLIMBED
TO THE TOP OF THE EMPIRE STATE BUILDING.
That's the same year that first ape ascended
the Empire State, made a celluloid ass of himself
over a blonde,
and we've all behaved perfectly disgraceful
over sex or the lack of it at one time.
But I've never climbed a skyscraper.
Oh, Frank O'Hara, we love you, get down.

The Poet, Before He Died

was very old,
but not too old

to touch my breast.
"I like the shape of it,"

he said. "The world
isn't round,

but deep," I answered.
Then he showed me depths

I didn't know
an old poet capable of.

Some might call this love,
but whatever it was,

I had come to trust the lines
his hands made

across my bare navel,
like roses in December

or a falling star,
barely glanced.

Grief by any other name,
smells like poetry.

Mercy Is for the Dogs

An elderly, arthritic Lassie
died peacefully
in her trainer's embrace
shortly after the needle
pierced heroic fur.

In the old days, animal benevolence
leagues used gas
to allay the hungry strays
so they would not die
roving the streets, starving.

Here in the twenty-first century,
with the abortion pill,
death penalty,
and war after war after war,
Dr. Kevorkian's a criminal.

His brand of Rx wouldn't raise any
judge's antiquated gavel
if the patients he tended
were Fido, Princess, or Rex.
But it's not for our wrecks of humanity,

not for the bloated, morphined masses
(our loved ones) who lie more dead than alive;
not for the writhing, too weak to writhe,
pained, fragile aged, mostly deaf, blind,
who've no joy left but for mindless sleep.

Mercy is for the dogs,
for the under-creatures, while we human
overlord species, managers of justice
must endure suffering—all sorts—
the price of knowledge, of mastery.

Recall this:
in the end, Travis
broken hearted, finds the courage, slays
Old Yeller with a single shot of his gun.
It is the only merciful way.

After "Finding a Long Gray Hair"

After Jane Kenyon

Using kinetic brush energy,
circular rhythms,
my face close to the floor
scrubbing, I shine.

Those wise old folk wives knew
how to get whiter whites
how to sing the blues—

Nothing lasts us but trouble and dirt.

And words—words that catch
under the ragged edges
of fingernails as we enact
this charge of womanhood.

I discover a ritual thread
under the fridge, a long gray hair,
kinky as the barbed wire
that is memory—

I am the keeper of my grandmother's mop.

When I am laid to rest,
the crescent reflection of the moon
off a wash pail
full of soapy water

in another woman's night kitchen,
is the only memorial need be lit.
Nothing last us, or outlasts us,
but trouble and dirt.

Did It Come True?

Start with a funeral:
priest in white robe, sandals,
waving a clanking censer
before crucifixion-
sized crosses,
pallbearers trailing the
dead weight of the casket
to the hearse;

the salesman uncle spewing
directions to the cemetery:
Hang right at the light,
eleven miles past Taco B's,
hang a louie.

Some will go wrong,
others will go home.

The widow in a limo
first time in her life,
not what she thought,
Wide turns make me dizzy.
She'd lower the window
if she could find a lever,
a switch.

The day is warm, overcast,
the ground cool.
No one minds
what no one minds.
Some crows caw.

Here is where and
no where else.
A little solipsism, a little peace.

Passing mourners observe
a toddler in denim coveralls

riding his daddy's shoulders up the block,
drooling, giggling,
lollipop bobbing like a baton,
a cartoon moon.

Where is the moon now?
someone wonders.

Where is the dead man,
where is your first love,

and where did that dream go,
the one you had
the night after your first kiss?

Was it a good one,
remember?

Morning Order for the Writer

After Billy Collins' "Night Letter to the Reader"

You must slip back between smoothed sheets,
a snake slithering beneath its rock,
a turtle entering its shell,

so that you will lie there, in the bed,
an extraordinary lethargist
amid the weave of cotton and polyester blend.

If you were older, you might be obsessing
over something you said at a meeting
about the common pedestrian,

or the freedom of Thursday mornings,
but as it is, you are complexly unconscious,
a person in a woolly sweater,

unable to sense all the bright desiccations
of the day and the mighty gales
that rail against even the lowliest shrubs.

The cat has preceded you into the bed,
and is curled nearby your head,
his nose, twitching as if he were about to sneeze,

owing to a thin layer of microbial dust,
invisible this morning on the boldly-colored coverlet,
and there is something else you must be told,

something about the cool green shade
in the stairwells of your dreams,
but now you are wondering if we are even speaking

and why you bother to listen to us about things
that will always change everything,
glacial ice, oceans of lava.

This is not what you want to be happening—
hear us sermonize that down on the plains
thousands of flute thrushes are struck mute—

threads coarse and warm against your cheeks,
and that, in every moment, the sun,
intense as a lens from Stephen King's

infamous eyeglasses, cools
rather inevitably, and will eventually
darken our entire indolent sky.

How to Fix a Flat

Love—is anterior to Life—
Posterior—to Death—
Initial of Creation, and
The Exponent of Earth—

— EMILY DICKINSON

Because God Doesn't Have Wings

he's jealous of his angels,
how they fly about creation
without fear of falling.

God is a trapeze artist
who always
relies on the net.

He twirls, pivots,
extends his arms as if wing bone—
the vacuum fails to uphold him.

God screams bloody
Light.
And so it is. He shouts again—

into being spring
solar winds, oxygen, the breath of
a lover the morning she leaves.

Catch me, God cries.
And the earth appears,
blue pail of water,

you here are on it, hidden
in the hydrangea bush, leaf-still,
your butterfly net poised.

Trapped

When the elevator stops between floors,
the woman in the grey suit,
with pinching red heels
and hair lacquered shut,
dreams the same dream
as the dough-faced messenger boy,
sweat already beading his upper lip, manila envelope
turning to oatmeal in his nervous fingers.

Together they fly about the tiny cage,
a mismatched pair of parakeets
awaiting the sweet old lady in the tea-stained apron
to pull off the cloth and call forth the day,
the way a magician pulls one rabbit after another
out of the same impossibly small hat,
or rejoins the severed halves of a woman
making her again whole.

Algebra

4 women
of 3 generations
are walking along
2nd Street together
in the rain
without any number
of umbrellas.

There is 1
red rose
in full bloom
by a blue mailbox
at the corner of 5th Ave.
The crosswalk light
is yellow.

It is 6 PM
Wednesday,
August 7th.
For how long
do these 4 women
stop
to inhale the smell?

Circumference: A Love Poem

$x = 2\pi r$
is what circulates

but does not equal
what's in my heart—

your smile that goes on
forever, irrational.

A relationship traverses
linear space,

finite
like everything

except the irrational—
π and your smile

upon seeing me come near.
And we can speak of area,

the space inside,
$y = \pi r^2$

as finite even though,
like love, it contains

the infinite, the irrational.
You are gone now.

Experts go on solving π
(they haven't seen your smile)

farther and farther out
and it will never be

enough,
nevereverneverevernevereverneverevernever . . .

How to Fix a Flat

1. Begin by looking up to the beech branch from which a black spider is threading his way to your open mouth.

1. Begin where open theory perches, a sparrow on the brown branch of shoulder.

1. Begin where tires spin on the muddy shoulder of the back road and the car will not progress.

1. Begin at the toll booth of the egress over the invisible line of division.

1. Begin at the scenic overlook, the distant hips of the mountains dewy with the new day.

1. Begin by facing east, the small golden hoop earring of the sun glinting into the shallow rocky riverbed.

1. Begin by skipping as a stone the maximum number of times.

1. Begin with a question, *how many jelly beans fill this jar?*

1. Begin on the back of a fly hovering over some jelly beans, his hairy haunches itching your palms.

1. Begin by opening and closing your fingers over and over like antennae trying to tune in.

1. Begin by listening to the light of stars and take mental notes.

1. Begin with the snowbound silence of a single blank page.

Snow

For Cecilia Woloch

After twenty inches
you let go the ruler,
the clock,
even the year.

You remember the work
your legs are capable of,
how toes
become frozen ghosts.

The world is once again
sun-time
and shadow, provisions
to be acquired before dark.

The mulled evening
is best spent
beside a leaping fire
that unchills breast and bone,

recalling your first glacial night,
when, disquieted
and marveling
at all the falling stars,

a single, glistering flake
skirted into your mouth,
melted on your startled tongue
as prayer.

Waiting

Sometimes
what you wait for
keeps you waiting
for so long
it seems like forever

and you have to
go on
anyway,
missing it,
feeling
abandoned,
lonely,
and stupid,

or just
angry at the world.

And nothing helps.

Not the rain
that patters
against the leaves.

Not the sun
that warms your knees.

Not even the song
suddenly
on the radio
from when you
were fifteen
and in love

with someone who
for five whole minutes
loved you back.

Nothing.

The phone rings
and you answer it.

Milk runs out
and you buy more.

By lunchtime
you forget
the dream

where your grandmother
brought you fresh cinnamon cookies.

At night
the moon's bleary face
watches you
through the blinds.

Later it's windy
and the trees
sound like
they're whispering.

You listen hard,
long after
the air goes dead,

until you comprehend
the special message
meant just for you.

It's another one of destiny's jokes
with that same punch line:

what you want
is long gone—
stop
waiting.

Summer Solstice

It harkens back to that first
Summer after kindergarten,
thinking how *my real life
has finally started—I'm a big
school girl now!* I spent
that July and August on edge,
reading every book from
the library's lower shelves,
getting sunburned in the grass,
yearning for September. And once
it came and I was back in the
classroom, I marveled how
daylight outside the tall old
windows told stories of other
lives, how the big wall
calendar's pages tore off and off,
blowing grade after grade into
history. It wasn't long before
I discovered division left messy
remainders, spelling lists held
absolute, disaster, necessary.
By eleven, I concluded—
most of life is grief. Now
past forty, I know the only
possible life is this—the inhaled
breath that comes on like Summer,
like light, and goes off
with each exhale
into a darkness that will
someday sooner than I can ever
imagine become permanent.

Walking, Late October

The skin you've been wearing
all these years is cold again
and you realize Summer's
become a postcard
too late to send.

The rent is due,
your account is low,
and the ground seems
harder with each step.

Near dusk the sun's bold,
the breeze and the light liquefy
leaves, waves from high
in the trees roll over you, a rush
of rosy gold.

If you were a fish, not a man,
you would drown in all that
false promise plain air is.
Fool's gold—what men died for
in the mountains; fools for gold—
the immigrants' American dreams
till their feet met
the unremarkable pavement.

You are a man, not a fish,
can't imagine life in water,
the constant buoyancy,
the constant cold your flesh
would be engineered not to feel.

You want to feel something
even if it's only this brisk wind, this
light and sun, and too much
to do and do and never be done.

Today it is darker than
it was yesterday at this time.
Soon you will set your watch back
to compensate, and that hour
will happen inside your dreams, wasted.

This walking is a kind of waking
dream, late October when birds
are scarce and car tires spin faster,
squirrels running fierce with nuts
not even pausing to eye you.

If this were a dream you'd be heading
somewhere important,
the final exam or the big dance,
then panic realizing you haven't studied,
or are wearing all the wrong clothes
if you've got any on at all.

But you're already awake, shivering,
and the panic you're feeling
feels misplaced, wordless,
as keys in hand, you spot your car
exactly where you thought you'd parked it,
cold matriculating into your cells.

Coltrane's "Soul Eyes"

beneath midnight's tongue
      your skin becomes smoke
         the gray curl of tenor sax
blowing your blood into violet dew

you hold hands with the Pleiades
those soulful sisters dancing blue-ice rhythm
into the sky   they whirl up their silvery skirts
      liquid cool   hot streams of Jack Daniels
and 'ol Jim tattoo gold into the throat of the instrument
      that brassy one that bends wind around
         the fleshy man   whose heart is loam
the man the very sound   of human creation

the universe begins in that starry dribble of spittle
      on his after-hour lips
explodes into notes   rain   apples   pre-blood pumping
stillness of a longing that snakes
         its way into your pipes

when he begins to blow
      slithers around your belly   predator
         the kind you are
prey   your body   hunter
     ambition   steam
rising through   your head
         made of straw

blowing into the moonglow
of a sad/funny world   of shoes hammers   briefcases
     rising up to the mouth of that giant angel
      the god who told you
      there would be light
         kissed you with his raspy lips
then set you down
      into the dark
         naked
           wet
and unalone

Sweet Stalk

An Elegy for Gwendolyn Brooks

hereafter
my cunning companion
we cool to grace
chase gray cares
above washed prayers
stroke the heaven place
mad
& bold
hunt the night to breaking

no sleek smoke
no crazy light

only the old
sad quiet
so soft
I must kiss
every milk sense
through untamed color
leap across tiger sleep
climb home
through long black to pillow

your absent ever
brave face

The Dead Man and Haystacks

After Marvin Bell

1. The Dead Man at Haystack Rock, Oregon, July 2006

The Dead Man knows Haystack Rock is not one of the eight wonders of the world.

Still, he half-expected (his alive half) that it would be like another World's Biggest Kielbasa in Chicopee or Half Dog-Half Deer outside Des Moines.

Roadside attractions and tourist destinations often turn out to be the way some enterprising folks bilk the low-intellect Americans of their not-so-hard-earned bucks.

The Kielbasa wasn't much bigger than a picnic table.

The half and half dog simply had a bobbed tail and graceful stature.

But Haystack Rock takes the Dead Man by surprise, he who's seen so many rocks, above and below ground.

If he were a pre-teen he'd dub it, *Awesome.*

At his wizened age, whatever that is, the Dead Man calls it, *Awesome.*

Despite all the photos, postcards, and paintings of it—its presence in person is inspiring.

The scale, he thinks it must be, or maybe that old Hebrew notion of the rock as God.

Whatever it is, it feels good sometimes to feel small.

With a perfection such as Haystack Rock before you, it lessens the burden of having to try to be so perfect all the time.

It becomes obvious how fool-hardy the quest for perfection is for anyone, especially the Dead Man.

2. The Dead Man at Chailly, Sunrise 1865

The Dead Man finds himself in front of the most gargantuan haystack he's ever seen—hay not rock.

The sun has already climbed midway, so that the haystack casts its shadow over him.

The Dead Man is confused.

He knows he was just in Oregon, thinking about the shape of the stone and how it reminded him of something else he'd seen.

The Dead Man notices there's something odd about this place.

The sky seems to be comprised of tiny dots of paint.

The haystack too, the green ground, the shadow, the distant blue mountains, all dots of paint.

Am I in need of glasses, am I going blind, is this a seizure? the Dead Man wonders.

Just as the Dead Man is about to faint with worry, he remembers Monet, *the painting.*

This is the one that Monet painted before all the others.

It took Monet 25 more years to do that famous series of wheatstacks.

This is the haystack that started it all.

The Dead Man realizes he is standing inside the painting.

The Dead Man checks to see if he is also made of tiny dots of paint.

He is not.

Somehow the notion of art has transported him inside it.

The Dead Man decides Monet's obsession with the scale and proportion and color of haystacks was more than justified but he wonders about the 25 years of not painting haystacks.

Triptych of Heaven

After three paintings by Edward Hopper

I. *Rooms by the Sea,* 1931

Heaven, this waking to the sea outside your door,
pale-butter light from the eastern sky
slathering the floor and walls
of the entryway. Heaven, this sight of
waves kissing up in crests, foam, fizzing.
Your eyes adjust to brilliance, your nose,
tickled by the air's salty breath.
An appetite rises deep within you,
for this day and all its hungry spaces to fill.
Terns cry out, their divining bodies
seize mouthfuls of silver
from liquid blue fields.

II. *Corn Hill, Truro, Cape Cod* 1930

At noon, the houses of Corn Hill are transformed
to haloed angels, and dune grass glows
with light that can only be limned as gold fire.
The air scented with *rugosa,*
dasya elegans, and goldenrod
feathers your skin with gooseflesh.
This sloping belly of bright earth,
this lambent heaven illumes
everything in aureate splendor,
thrilling your senses completely, so that here, now,
you become ecstasy and delirium,
you are everywhere, and infinite, and dazzling.

III. *The Long Leg,* 1935.

Near dusk, the sky is as great as all prayer.
Sails push clouds back,
your tiny sailboat slides along like a smooth bead

on the throat of the crushed-sapphire sea.
Wind-bruised, the mouth of the water
sings to the rocks at land's edge.
You, dizzy on new legs, hear its voice,
"I give you back," it sings, "I give you back."
As darkness falls, you search like the distant lighthouse,
profoundly in awe of stars, of traveling vessels,
of the ocean that your heart is,
what your life on earth provides—heaven.

Clothesline Life

After viewing Nancy E. B. Shibles' photo "Laundry and Light"

Four button-down shirts pinned across
the line in waves swing upside down,
diaphanous, other-worldly
in the afternoon sun filtered by cumulus.
They could be mammoth pale tulip petals,
or the shed skin of angels.

The shadows cast upon the ground
by dangling shirt sleeves
become chair legs,
shirt hems are the heads
of comfortably seated tea-party guests,
you bring the cups, real or imaginary.

Isn't mother just inside the house,
baking from scratch,
an egg-basted loaf
to accompany a dinner of roast beef
and glazed carrots?

And won't father
be pulling into the driveway
right at six o'clock,
the old Buick's tires crunching
the gravel like ribbon candy?

In this clotheslined backyard:
long-tailed kites
swooping and diving through bright air,
children running barefoot
through cool lawn sprinklers,
trees old as grandparents
casting shade-castles,
reprieve from August's blaze.

This is a place of suspended laundry,
suspended time,
Summer, forever
unfolding.

Tonight,
wish upon the first star you see
that this clothesline life
you didn't grow up with,
through the grace of a photograph,
imprints itself on your heart,
so that wherever you are you remember
the scent of breeze-clean laundry.

Screen Door To the Sea

After the painting by James B. Wyeth

Was it the insistent wallpaper roses?

Was it the sepia light inside the house,
that shadowed sadness
into a young boy's face,
his waistcoat black as dread,
his nervous thumbs pressed together
as if he wanted to ask
but couldn't?

The boy went to find an answer
just beyond the screen door,
where the green sea groans
murky disapproval
and the blue sky promises
impossible things.

The clock forever stopped at seven minutes to twelve.

Adaptation in the Motor City

Goldfinches thrive in the Detroit airport,
dart and dive in and out of startlingly life-like
Ash, Birch, and Balsam, singing.

A blonde woman in heels taller
than her skirt is long,
spikes along the slippery linoleum,
gingerly rolling her bags.

A sixtyish man with loosened tie,
open collar bellows sales projections
into his cell phone headset.

A grim-reaper-tattooed teenager
with four satchels and a latte
argues with the wing-pinned gate clerk
he's the exception to the two-carry-on rule.

A bald lady in a wheelchair, tubes feeding
oxygen through her pinched nostrils,
tells a pilot a joke and both laugh uncontrollably.

What Mr. Darwin failed to note:
the definitive mechanism
of human adaptation
is hope.

The Paradox of Life and Religion

Pearls never heat up
purer than time
that slip of a girl bare-armed as summer
who next chance you look
is as rugged as relief maps of the Alps

Switch to whole
milk, saintly cheeses
the voice of prayer
and tiny cobalt blue bottles
of evening in Paris

Lace scallops too much of the world,
yellows   tears away from edges

Hammer the holy spirit in place
measure the crush of your tin heart
by its chime
make votives of rusty chain
        hymnals of your old school medals
in your polished shoes
plane tree bark   down to its roots

A mold can be made for anything
        the sound of the wind through sand dunes
        teeth that chattered on an April day, too cold
        a cross too weighty not to bear

It isn't safe to assume
showy plumage speaks for the bird

Wax wings succumb
and the Minotaur weeps

This life is
a double-boil
fire concealed below
all white-glove inspections

Insulated
even a thin wick can spark

the sea's voice
a single shell   finite basket of ocean
is magic enough

Hold up to your ear
the idea of centuries
swimming between the unbroken seams of
original nest
paradise of caviar and fins

Even for whales Christmas came much later
cookie-cut from the candied bread of sorrow
Yeats never made it to Mardi Gras
and next Wednesday is a week away
despite a four-leaf clover
burning its green door in your pocket

My advice: roll up your bandage
pride flesh stings even when kissed
by the lips of Spring air

Desire can explode
the leather off a softball
every time

Intention's as unexacting
as chopsticks to the uninitiated Caucasian

Rest your spine
Rest your mandible
Rest your eyelashes
Listen to the origami sound of
moth wings bumping bumping
bumping against the stove-hot bulb

he's giving his all for faith
for illumination

giving his all for this poem
and it doesn't matter
it doesn't matter

just say *"Jean d'Arc"*

Sestina

After Elizabeth Bishop

The art of sestina is hard.
Bishop who chose all nouns to end
her lines must have intended the stove
to be heavy with metaphor, the house
so full of loss, even the almanac
wept moon tears. In the face of such loss, we are all children

coloring in the grief-white pages, children
and grandmothers busying ourselves with singing, listening too hard
for the inevitable kettle's scream. The almanac
time keeps is inscrutable, everything moving toward its end,
time to sow, to reap, to bury. The garden in a child's drawing of a house
is ever-blooming, the man is always at home. Meanwhile, the stove

of the heart heats, cools. The re-stoked furnace stove
in the basement grumbles, ghostly, frightening children
who have yet to learn how natural losing is. The rigid symbol of house
stands for haven, shelter, safety, the impossibly hard
umbrella for life's rains. But the man, alluded to in a drawing, his end,
his fate, is unknown. Perhaps the well-worn almanac

failed to foretell that day's September rain—the tarot-almanac,
the hanging fool, death card suspended upended over the black stove,
not a songbird at all, but a raven, a harbinger of endings.
Only the stone balloon of the moon shrinks and re-inflates, children
and grandmothers alike clamor for similar miracle. But truth is hard,
and hardly ever given voice. The teakettle speaks it in this house,

its tears tiny shrieks dancing to death on the stove. This is a house
with a secret everybody knows, especially the clever almanac
obsessed with time tables, the same tired jokes: laughter comes hard,
and always at great cost. Grandmother singing, slaving at her stove,
knows this. Having drawn a man with tears for buttons, even the child
knows this but does not yet know she knows how inevitable are endings.

The sestina is another attempt to master endings
by not letting them end. Rain beats on the roof of its house
of words, end-words drops in the water cycle, going round and round: a
    child's
game—*Pocketful of poesies, ashes, ashes, we all fall* and we do. The almanac's
tables overflow: rain, ground water, rivers, tea-water sputtering on the stove.
The kettle comes to full boil, the equinoctial whistle sounds: life is hard.

Time to plant tears, says the almanac. A flower bed's soft earth goes winter-
    hard.
Grandmother's stove warns: *sip those dark tears, a sober tea—sweet child-
    hood ends*
abruptly. Sestinas are the dream-houses where words shun rain, play on and
    on.

What the Roof Hears at Night

It is the voice of the farm wife,
at her kitchen sink, scouring pans,
singing a song of her mother,
and her mother's mother before,
a plain, honest voice that expands
to fill drafty places, those leaky dikes
two hundred-year-old clapboards are,
upheld more by stubbornness than repair.

It is her singing, stirring the mice
from their slumber between the walls,
reliable alarm alerting them to the fall
of evening, time for plunder and play.
They scurry on their small, brown paws
with such quiet care, so as to cause
no disturbance as they make their way
to the pantry's staple sacks of flour and rice.

From the living room, in the easy chair,
the husband, heavy with evening meal,
heavy with sleep, slumps chin to chest,
his snores, thick with alcohol, snores
full of chain and grumbling gears,
human echo of his workday's chores.
The television gabs, guffaws, squeals
incessantly, a most thoughtless guest.

Upstairs, on the son's bed, the ancient hound
curls around to a moth-chewed teddy bear.
The son, gone without telling anyone where,
will not be home tonight, or soon, to sound
the requisite scolding for jumping up on furniture
(not his own idea of course, but his father's decree).
Resting in forbidden comfort, the dog wheezes,
his breath slows, a steady rhythm ripples his fur.

And still, it is the farm wife's voice, her song increasing,
dispersing to cobwebs where restive spiders spin
demise for the houseflies; and even into the crevices
her careful dust-mop misses go the words her kin
taught her to sing while laboring, words severed
from meaning or thought, the back of her throat
rousing them to a nearly unbearable sweetness
till she can sing no more, and a sigh is her final note.

Last Night

I stopped to look
at that cracked teacup
moon in the sky,
nothing I
hadn't seen before—
suddenly
the thought—
what if
from a distant vantage
across this expansive
universe,
for a stranger
who just happens
to look our way,
each fractured
one of us
shines?

About the Title

YEARS AGO, when I lived in New Hampshire, I found myself traveling along State Road 103 through the tiny hamlet of Newbury and came upon what locals call *Chicken Rock*. Chicken Rock is a brownish-gray granite boulder a few feet back from the road, and to my recollection, approximately six feet high and twice as wide and deep. Painted on the front of the boulder in thick white letters were the words, "Chicken Farmer I Still Love You." I was intrigued and moved by this brazen message of love, and went on to write a poem about this message.

Later, as I began forming my collection around this poem, I looked into the background of the mysterious Chicken Rock. Apparently the rock is famous, having been written up in *Yankee Magazine* as a "Best Love Story of 1997" and in *Chicken Soup for the Couples Soul*. According to Newbury town librarian, Rosina Johnson, the writer of this enduring declaration of love is still unknown. But with Rosie's help, and the assistance of local photographer, Maureen Rosen, I was able to piece together this much of the story.

More than thirty years ago there lived a family in town who raised chickens and had a small egg business. One of the members of the family, a lovely young daughter, was the one who inspired in her anonymous admirer this public display of affection. His message was originally spray-painted on the rock and it read, "Chicken Farmer I Love You."

Years passed, the message faded, and vegetation grew up around the boulder. But suddenly, seemingly overnight, the vegetation was removed and a new message appeared on the boulder, "Chicken Farmer I Still Love You." No one knows if the original writer returned to make a declaration of his continued and undying love, or if it was someone new who painted it.

Sometime later, in 1997, someone reported the new message as graffiti and it was painted over by the highway department. The citizens of Newbury felt "great consternation" that their "valued and historic legend" had been lost. So they put together a petition, signed by 192 of the residents, and sent it to the highway department asking them to restore the message and let it stand. The petition included the following statements:

". . . and Whereas that message, declaring CHICKEN FARMER I STILL LOVE YOU has become a valued and historic legend in the Town, and Whereas that message has uplifted the spirits of travelers along Route

103 for more than twenty years, and Whereas the impact of that message has been entirely positive during its lifetime . . . Now, therefore, we the Selectmen of the Town of Newbury in the State of New Hampshire do hereby respectfully request the Commissioner of the Department of Transportation to let this message of love, faith, and endurance stand on the ledge on Route 103 in the Town of Newbury."

The petition was approved, the message repainted, and it will be maintained as a tribute not only to "faith, love, and endurance," but to the human spirit of hope that permeates one small town in New Hampshire, and I believe, is alive in all of us, from wherever we hail.

About the Author

LANA HECHTMAN AYERS, originally from New York, spent fifteen years in New England before relocating to the Seattle area where she is a manuscript consultant, writing workshop leader, poetry editor of the *Crab Creek Review* and publishes the *Concrete Wolf Poetry Chapbook Series*. She holds a degree in Theoretical Mathematics, a Masters in Counseling Psychology and an MFA in Poetry. She hopes someday to return to school to study Astrophysics.

Although, she'd been writing poems for many years, it was not until the Spring of 1987 that her life as a poet began. It was then she attended a poetry workshop led by Ottone "Ricky" Riccio at the Boston Center for Adult Education. She entered the classroom with a two-page "masterpiece" and left with about five salvageable lines. She studied with Ricky for over a decade and considers him a mentor in the purest sense: he is able to greet each poet on the threshold of the poem and welcome them in. After Ricky, Lana was fortunate enough to study with equally gifted mentor, Patricia Fargnoli, whose faith in her gave her the courage to pursue an MFA. Lana also credits poet Kate Gleason's workshops with opening her inner voice.

Lana's first book, *Dance From Inside My Bones*, won Snake Nation Press' Violet Reed Haas Award and is currently nominated for the National Book Award. This is her second full-length poetry collection.

For more on this author, please visit her website at http://LanaAyers.com.